Bugs, Bees, and other Buzzy Creatures

DK | Penguin Random House

Senior editor **Wendy Horobin**
Editorial assistant **Sophia Danielsson-Waters**
Senior designer **Claire Patané**
Designer **Charlotte Bull**
Design assistants **Eleanor Bates, Rachael Hare**
Photographer **Ruth Jenkinson**
Producer **Leila Green**
Producer, Pre-Production **Andy Hilliard**
Jacket designer **Charlotte Bull**
Jacket coordinator **Francesca Young**
Creative technical support **Sonia Charbonnier**
Managing editor **Penny Smith**
Managing art editor **Gemma Glover**
Art director **Jane Bull**
Publisher **Mary Ling**

First published in Great Britain in 2016 by
Dorling Kindersley Limited
80 Strand, London WC2R 0RL

Copyright © 2016 Dorling Kindersley Limited
A Penguin Random House Company
10 9 8 7 6 5 4 3 2 1
001–285433–Mar/16

A CIP catalogue record for this book is available
from the British Library.
ISBN: 978-0-2412-3102-9
Printed in China.
All images © Dorling Kindersley Limited
For further information see: www.dkimages.com

A WORLD OF IDEAS
SEE ALL THERE IS TO KNOW

www.dk.com

Parents

This booked is packed with activities for your little ones to enjoy. We want you all to have a great time, but please be safe and sensible – especially when you're doing anything that might be dangerous (or messy!) Have fun.

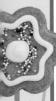

2

Contents

Let's count legs

Bugs come in all **shapes** and **sizes**.

You can often tell which **type** you are

looking at by counting its legs.

Six legs

6

If a creature has six legs, say hello to an insect! All insects have six legs. Bees, beetles, and ants are insects.

Eight legs

How many legs does this one have?

8

Can you count eight legs? If so, you are looking at a spider or scorpion. They always have eight legs.

Shake a leg

Insect legs are not just for walking and running. They use them for jumping, climbing, swimming, digging, holding their food, and making noises.

No legs

Slugs don't have any legs, but they do have a foot.

Worms move by wriggling.

Lots of legs

20+

Centipedes have one pair of legs on each body segment. They can run very fast.

Hundreds of legs

Millipedes have short, stubby legs.

100+

One, two, three, four, five... too many legs to count? That's a millipede. Some have 750 legs!

5

Boxy bugs

You can make **all sorts of bugs** out of an egg box. Why not try a **spider** or a **caterpillar**?

You will need:
Egg boxes
Paint
Scissors
Pipe cleaners
Googly eyes

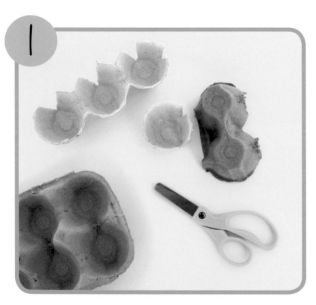

1

Ask an adult to cut the egg boxes into strips. Try one bump for a spider and two or three for a beetle. Use a long box for a caterpillar.

2

Paint your bug's body. If you like, you can add spots or stripes, or make each of the bumps a different colour.

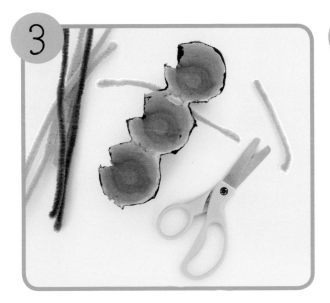

Ask an adult to cut pipe cleaners into equal lengths to make legs. Push them *between* the bumps, then *bend* the ends up into feet.

Twist some pipe cleaners around a pencil to make feelers and poke them into the head. Add eyes and a mouth, and you have a bug!

Wriggly caterpillars

Look closely at a plant and you may see a caterpillar **wriggling** up a stem or **chewing holes** in a leaf. Very soon it will change into something **amazing**.

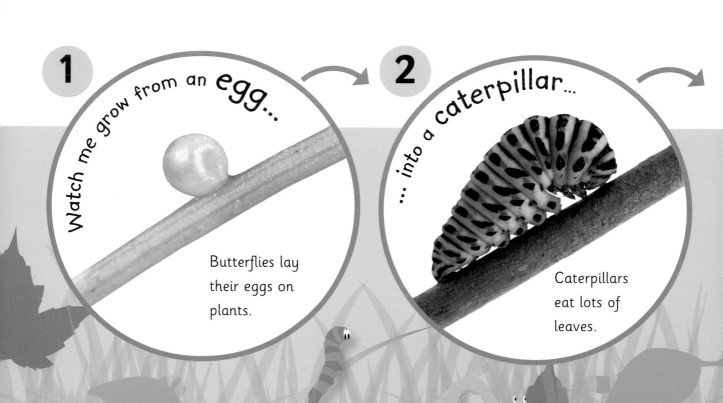

1 Watch me grow from an **egg**...

Butterflies lay their eggs on plants.

2 ...into a **caterpillar**...

Caterpillars eat lots of leaves.

Did you know?

Not all caterpillars become butterflies – some turn into moths.

3

...then a **chrysalis**...

A hard case protects the caterpillar while it is changing.

4

...and finally a **butterfly!**

Butterflies

Hang up these **butterflies**

so they can **flutter** in the wind.

You will need:
Cardboard tubes
Paints
Coloured paper
Scissors
Craft glue or sticky tape
Pipe cleaners
Googly eyes

Paint a cardboard tube and leave it to dry. This will be the body of your butterfly. While it's drying, make the wings.

Fold a piece of paper in half. Draw a capital "B" shape along the fold and cut around it. Open out the wings and decorate with card.

Apply a line of glue along the middle of the butterfly's body, then stick the cardboard tube to the wings and leave it to dry.

Twist two pipe cleaners around a pencil to make feelers and stick them on with tape. Add some eyes and draw on a friendly smile.

Tape thread to the back of your butterfly so you can hang it up.

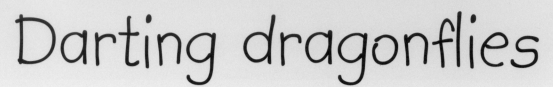
Darting dragonflies

See that? It's a **colourful dragonfly** flying over the **water** at **super speed**. If you blink you might just miss it!

Water birth

Dragonflies are born in water and live there for several years. This is why adult dragonflies are usually found by ponds, rivers, and lakes.

Dragonflies have long thin bodies and large heads.

Dragonfly babies are called nymphs.

Did you know?

Dragonflies are the most successful hunters in the insect world and almost always catch their prey.

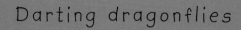

Fast fliers

These amazing acrobats use their two sets of large wings to fly at great speeds, change direction instantly, hover in place, and even fly backwards.

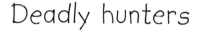

Deadly hunters

They may be pretty, but to other insects they're very scary. A dragonfly can eat a hundred flies and mosquitoes every day.

Dragonflies have huge eyes that let them see in different directions at the same time.

13

Dragonfly pegs

Use a **dizzy** dragonfly to keep your **bits and pieces** of paper neat and **tidy**.

You will need:
Clothes pegs
Paints and paintbrush
Coloured paper
Scissors
Coloured pens
PVA glue
Googly eyes

Paint a wooden clothes peg or decorate a coloured plastic one. This will be the body of your dragonfly.

Fold a piece of coloured paper in half and ask an adult to cut a rough heart shape to make a pair of wings. Decorate with paints or pens.

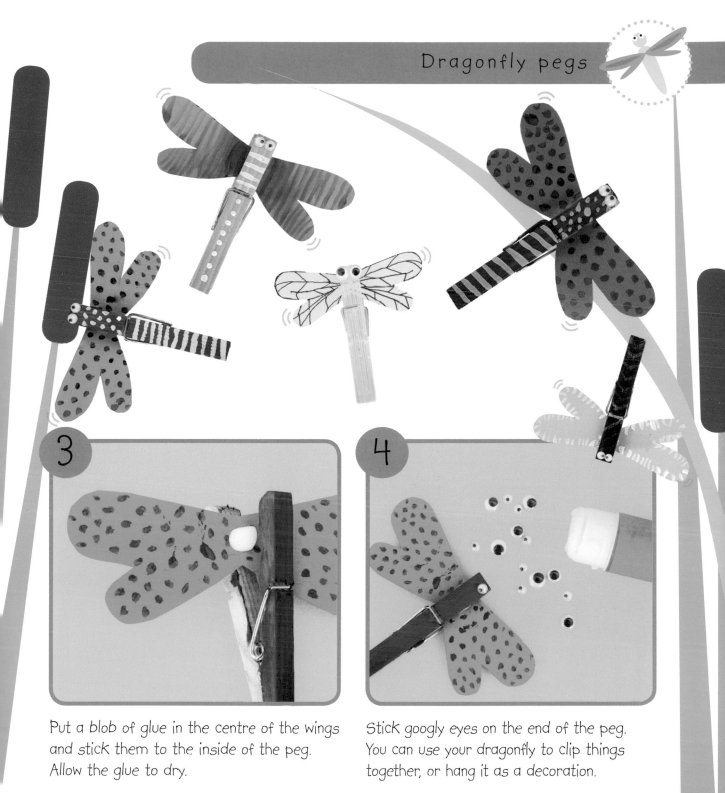

3

Put a *blob* of glue in the centre of the wings and *stick* them to the inside of the peg. Allow the glue to dry.

4

Stick googly eyes on the end of the peg. You can use your dragonfly to clip things together, or hang it as a decoration.

15

Hoppers and crickets

Grasshoppers and **crickets** are similar bugs that are known for **making noise** and **jumping around!**

Grasshoppers and crickets look similar, but crickets have shorter antennae. This is an easy way to tell them apart.

Did you know?
Crickets "sing", by rubbing their wings together to make a loud noise.

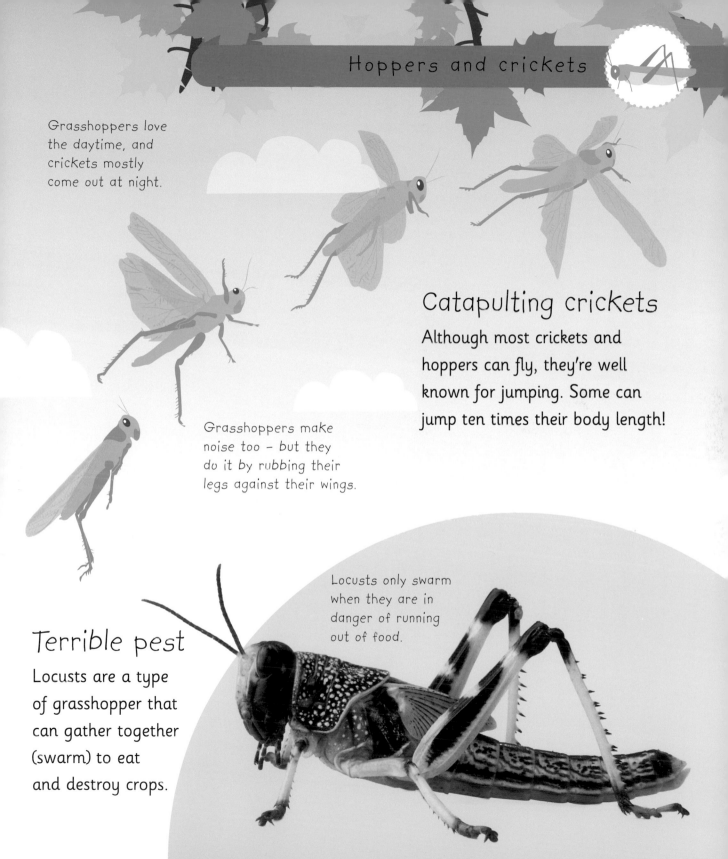

Grasshoppers love the daytime, and crickets mostly come out at night.

Catapulting crickets

Although most crickets and hoppers can fly, they're well known for jumping. Some can jump ten times their body length!

Grasshoppers make noise too – but they do it by rubbing their legs against their wings.

Locusts only swarm when they are in danger of running out of food.

Terrible pest

Locusts are a type of grasshopper that can gather together (swarm) to eat and destroy crops.

Buzzy bees

Bees are busy insects. Every day they fly off to collect **nectar** from hundreds of flowers, which they turn into sweet, golden honey.

Pollen basket

BUZZZZ

The buzzing noise is made by their wings when they fly.

Bumblebees

These plump, stripy bees have long, fuzzy hair all over their body. They have baskets on their back legs for collecting pollen.

Did you know?

It takes the nectar of two million flowers to make one pot of honey.

18

Honeybees

Honeybees live in large groups. Their nest is called a hive.

When a honeybee finds flowers with lots of nectar it does a waggle dance to tell the others where to find them.

BUZZZZ
BUZZZZ

Bees build six-sided wax "rooms" to store honey. Eating honey helps them survive through the winter.

Honeybees busy building a comb.

19

Honey biscuits

Become a **busy bee** **yourself** by making these **yummy** honey **flower** biscuits.

Ingredients
125 g (4½ oz) butter
125 g (4½ oz) caster sugar
1 tbsp honey
1 egg yolk
175 g (6 oz) plain flour
1 tsp cinnamon

1

Beat the butter and sugar together in a bowl until they are pale and creamy.

2

Next, add the honey and the egg yolk and mix together.

3

Sieve the flour and cinnamon into the bowl then mix until it forms a soft dough.

4

Sprinkle flour on a board and a rolling pin. Roll out the dough until it is 5 mm (¼in) thick.

5

Preheat the oven to 180°C (350°F/Gas 4). Cut out flower shapes with a cookie cutter.

6

Ask an adult to put the tray in the oven.

Place the biscuits on a tray and bake in the oven for 12–15 minutes until golden brown.

For the icing

100 g (3½ oz) icing sugar
3 tsp water
Piping bag
Sprinkles

1

Mix the icing sugar with the water to form a thick paste. Put it into a piping bag and decorate your biscuits.

Why not add some pretty sprinkles?

Brilliant beetles

You're never far from a **beetle**. Hiding under **leaves**, crawling, swimming or **flying**, they are almost everywhere!

You can find beetles in lots of colours.

Nearly half of all insects are beetles!

A hard, shiny casing protects beetle's wings.

Little and large

Some beetles are so teeny tiny they'll fit on a pin head. Others are giants, measuring around 20cm (8in) long.

Some beetles destroy trees and crops.

Did you know?

Beetles cannot see very well so they release special smells to communicate.

Did you know that ladybirds are beetles?

Lots of spots!

Ladybirds are **shiny**, round, spotted **beetles** that come in many colours. Let's see how many **spots** these ladybirds have.

...four...

4

Did you know that ladybirds can fly?

Two spots...

2

... six...

6

24 How many **ladybirds** can you count?

... seven...

7

Did you know?

The ladybird's bright colours warn birds that they are not nice to eat.

twenty-nine!...

29

...nineteen...

19

Ladybirds can have a few spots, many spots, or no spots at all. Some of them have stripes instead!

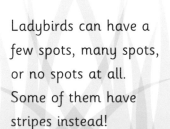

25

Ladybird pebbles

Create your **own family** of **little** ladybirds. All you need are **pebbles** and paint!

You will need:
Smooth, bug-shaped pebbles
Acrylic paint
Paintbrushes

1

Gather your pebbles and give them a good scrub. Once you've made sure they're nice and clean, dry them off.

2

Cover as much of the pebble as you can with black paint and leave it to dry. When it's ready, turn it over and paint the rest.

3

Paint oval-shaped wing cases on one side of the pebble. These are usually red, yellow, or orange. Let them dry then paint black spots.

4

Once the spots have dried, paint a friendly face on the front. Why not make more with a different number of spots?

Awesome ants

Ants are amazing insects. **Millions** of them live and work **together** to look after and **protect** their nest.

Leafcutter ants take leaves and flowers back to the nest for food.

Ants use their feelers to touch, taste, and smell.

28

One two, three, four...

When ants find food they leave a scent trail that leads other ants to the food.

Girl power

Most ants are female. They build the nest, protect it against invaders, and collect food for other ants.

Super ants

Ants are incredibly strong for their size. Some of them can lift objects that are more than 20 times their own weight.

Did you know?

There are thought to be one million ants for every human on Earth.

Ants often build their nests underground.

29

Amazing ant maze

Ants live in large groups called **colonies.** Many colonies have underground nests.

Can you find a path through the nest to the queen?

Start

Worker ants look after the nest and dig all the tunnels.

Nests have lots of rooms and tunnels.

The ants have lots of jobs such as looking after the larvae (babies).

Help the ant reach the queen

Not all colonies are built underground, some ants build nests in tree trunks.

Food is brought from outside and stored in large rooms.

The queen is the most important ant in the colony. She gets to have the biggest room!

Finish

31

Index

Acknowledgements

The publisher would like to thank the following
for their kind permission to reproduce their photographs:

(Key: a-above; b-below/bottom; c-centre; f-far; l-left; r -right; t-top)

5 Colin Keates (c) Dorling Kindersley, Courtesy of the Natural History
Museum, London (br). **12** Dreamstime.com: Andersastphoto (bl). **22**
Colin Keates (c) Dorling Kindersley, Courtesy of the Natural History
Museum, London (bl). **23** Fotolia: Eric Isselee (tcr); Fotolia: giuliano2022
(bcr); Dreamstime.com: Vladvitek (cr). **28** Dorling Kindersley: Thomas
Marent (bl). **30** naturepl.com: Ann & Steve Toon (cr); Visuals Unlimited
(br). **31** naturepl.com: Steven David Miller (cb).

All other images © Dorling Kindersley
For further information see: www.dkimages.com

Thanks to Lucy Claxton for picture library help, and
James Mitchem for editorial assistance.